I0802573

Introduction by W. Terrence Gordon

This, McLuhan's first published article, appeared in *The Dalhousie Review*, 15, 4 (1936), 455-64. Identifying Chesterton with the true mystics who reveal mysteries rather than obscuring them, McLuhan anticipates the basis of his own eventual approach to media, saying: "The mysteries revealed by Mr. Chesterton are the daily miracles of sense and consciousness." From his "more than ordinary awareness and freshness of perception," McLuhan states, Chesterton derived his "extraordinarily strong sense of fact," a sense that McLuhan also possessed and derived from the same source. In his teachings, McLuhan was to emulate the Chesterton who "consciously causes a clash between appearances in order to attract attention to a real truth transcending such a conflict." As for the cornerstone of McLuhan's thought, the transforming power of media, it emerges here (linked to language, which McLuhan would later call mankind's first technology for letting go of the environment in order to grasp it in new ways) as the compelling quality he identified in Chesteron, who "deserves the praise Mr. Eliot affords to Donne for the 'quality of transmuting ideas into sensations, of transforming an observation into a state of mind.'" — WTG

G. K. Chesterton: A Practical Mystic

Marshall McLuhan

When it is seen that there are two principal sides to everything, a practical and a mystical, both exciting yet fruitful, then the meaning and effect of Mr. Chesterton can become clear, even to those who delight to repeat that he stands on his head. That tireless vigilance in examining current fashion and fatalism, which has characterized him for more than thirty years, clearly depends upon his loyalty to a great vision: "His creed of wonder was Christian by this absolute test, that he felt it continually slipping from himself as much as from others." Therefore the prosaic is invariably the false appearance of things to fatigued intellect and jaded spirit. This is the basis of Mr. Chesterton's inspiriting opposition to the spread of officialdom and bureaucracy. The cynical social legislation of to-day, undertaken in supposed accord with unyielding economic circumstance, is often light-headed because it is not light-hearted. And Mr. Chesterton is a revolutionary, not because he finds everything equally detestable, but because he fears lest certain infinitely valuable things, such as the family and personal liberty, should perish. That Beauty transformed the Beast only because she loved it while it was yet a beast, is timelessly significant.

It is necessary to define the sense in which Mr. Chesterton is a mystic, before the relation of this to the practical side can be judged. He once wrote: "Real mystics don't hide mysteries, they reveal them. They set a thing up in broad daylight, and when you've seen it, it is still a mystery. But the mystagogues hide a thing in darkness and secrecy; and when you find it, it's a platitude." The mysteries revealed by Mr. Chesterton are the daily miracles of sense and consciousness. His ecstasy and gratitude are for what has been given to all men. He rejoices at "the green hair" on the hills, or "the smell of Sunday morning", and

> Those rolling mirrors made alive in me,
> Terrible crystal more incredible
> Than all the things they see.

Here it is possible only to speak of the sacramental sense of the life of earth and sea and sky, of tillage and growth, and of food and wine, which informs his work. For to him existence has a value utterly inexpressible, and absolutely superior to any arguments for optimism or pessimism. What truce could such a great lover of life make with agnostic humanitarianism and world-weary eugenists? To those "who have snarled through the ages" he hurls this reply:

> Know that in this grotesque old masque
> Too loud we cannot sing,
> Or dance too wild or speak too wide
> To praise a hidden thing.

It is the spirit of Christendom, as it was the spirit of R. L. Stevenson; but it is not the spirit of the age. In this sense Mr. Chesterton is reactionary. If universal nature made shipwreck to-morrow, yet would

> One wild form reel on the last rocking cliff,
> And shout: "The daisy has a ring of red."

Mr. Chesterton has stepped beyond the frontiers of poetry, to what M. Maritain in speaking of Rimbaud calls, "The Eucharistic passion which he finds in the heart of life."

As a comment on one of his characters, he wrote: "He had somehow made a giant stride from babyhood to manhood, and missed that crisis in youth when most of us grow old." Mr. Chesterton himself is full of that child-like surprise and enjoyment which a sophisticated age supposes to be able to exist only in children. And it is to this more than ordinary awareness and freshness of perception that we may attribute his extraordinarily strong sense of fact. We can apply to him what he wrote of a young poet in one of his stories: "What are to most men impressions or half impressions, were to him incidents... The slope of a hill or the corner of a house checked him like a challenge. He wrestled with it seriously, until he could put something like a name to his nameless fancy." This profound humility in the face of reality is the very condition of honest art and all philosophy, and it explains Mr. Chesterton's imaginative sympathy with popular legends and proverbs; just as it is the reason for his energetic revival of tradition in so far as it dignifies and illuminates any present activity. In short, he is original in the only possible sense, because he considers everything in relation to its origins. It is because he is concerned to maintain our endangered institutions that he earnestly seeks to re-establish agriculture and small property, the only basis of any free culture.

But most of all does his strong sense of fact account for the recurrence of seeming paradoxes in his writings:

> The more plain and satisfying our state appears, the more we may know we are living in an unreal world. For the real world is not satisfying. The more clear become the colours and facts of Anglo-Saxon superiority, the more surely we may know we are in a dream. For the real world is not clear or plain. The real world is full of bracing bewilderments and brutal surprises. Comfort is the blessing and the curse of the English... For there is but an inch of difference between the cushioned chamber and the padded cell.

All profound truth, philosophical and spiritual, makes game with appearances, yet without really contradicting common sense. That is why Mr. Chesterton accuses the Victorians of believing in real paradoxes, such as expecting all men to have the same morals when they had different religions, or supposing that it was practical to be illogical. A little attention shows how he consciously causes a clash between appearances in order to attract attention to a real truth transcending such a conflict. There is no hint or hue of meaning amidst the dizziest crags of thought that is safe from his swift, darting, pursuit. We return safely and lucidly from the exhilarating chase of an idea to its logical conclusion. Such a world, rigid with thought and brilliant with colour, is the very antithesis of the pale-pink lullaby-land of popular science. It is the difference between a cathedral window and blank infinity. That is why modern life, thoughtless and unpoised, has degenerated from a dance into a race, and history is regarded as a toboggan slide. But Mr. Chesterton has exposed the Christless cynicism of the supposedly iron laws of economics, and has shown that history is a road that must often be reconsidered and even retraced. For, if Progress implies a goal, it does not imply that all roads lead to it inevitably. And to-day, when the goal of Progress is no longer clear, the word is simply an excuse for procrastination.

It is scarcely necessary now, when philosophy and art have been revitalised by the study of medieval achievements, to explain that Mr. Chesterton does not want "to go back to the middle ages", and never did. "There is none rides back to pick up a glove or a feather." But the merest reference to anything prior to the Reformation starts a clock-work process in the mind of the nineteenth century journalists who still write most of our papers: "Mr. Chesterton is a medievalist; and he is therefore quite justified (from his own benighted standpoint) in indulging as he does in the sport of tearing out the teeth of Jews, burning hundreds of human beings alive, and perpetually seeking for the Philosopher's Stone." Without these automatic and irresponsible reactions to anything resembling serious thought, there could not be that vast and increasing mountain of printed paper which indicates that progress is proceeding. For, as Stevenson noted, man lives not by bread alone, but by catchwords also. It all began with Luther's anathemas against Reason, and Descartes's expressed contempt for Aristotle and Aquinas.

The conspiracy, hatched at that time, to ignore history, which in practice meant the middle ages, had not been generally found out when Mr. Chesterton began to write. Certainly he knew there must have been something right about centuries whose architectural remains were admired by every class of mind. He was absolutely certain that people who were capable of an intensely significant use of colours, whose dress was as many-hued as the walls and windows of their churches, could not be as black as they were painted. So much he had in common with Ruskin, Rossetti and Morris; but much deeper was his interest in the origins of that magnificent and complex culture. His was the intellectual interest of Newman rather than the aesthetic interest of Burne-Jones. "If we want the flowers of chivalry, we must go back to the roots of chivalry, Theology." And since it is always the world of ideas that determines the climate of sensation and opinion, the Troubadors, and Dante, and the Metaphysicals are to-day throbbing again with vital interest for us. Similarly the moral atmosphere of the Victorian time was prepared by Locke and Bentham, and, though inchoate, had stirred the anger of Keats:

> Fools! Make me whole again that weighty pearl
> The Queen of Egypt melted, and I'll say
> That ye may love in spite of beaver hats.

Now Mr. Chesterton has never written a book to praise the Middle Ages, but he has written books to praise and explain the life of St. Francis and the thought of Aquinas. For, as he explains, "real conviction and real charity are very much nearer than men suppose." It is plain that he is literally a radical, because he goes to the roots of things. And it is for that reason that he is very hopeful for this generation, which has been forced back to roots and origins. Thus because it is sceptical even about scepticism, "the sophisticated youth, who has seen through the sophistical old men, may even yet see something worth seeing."

Although Mr. Chesterton has never entertained any desire to restore the Middle Ages, he shows that certain timeless principles were then understood which have since been foolishly forgotten. Though they were not the right place, they were the right turning, and subsequent history has in a deep sense been an ignoble retreat from their difficult and untried ideas. It was a rout which distorted and diminished the Renaissance, and nullified its proud promises to us. Mr. Chesterton's concentration on history has been a splendid effort to rescue a civilization weakened by capitalism from the logical conclusion of capitalism, which is, either the servile or the communistic State:

> The highest use of the imagination is to learn from what never happened. It is to gather the rich treasures of truth stored up as much in what never was as in what was and will be. We are accused of praising and even idealising retrograde and barbaric things. What we praise is the progress which was for those retrograde things prevented, and the civilization that those barbarians were not allowed to reach. We do not merely praise what the Middle Ages possessed. It would be far truer to say that we praise . . . what they were never al-

lowed to possess. But they had in them the potentiality of the possession; and it was *that* that was lost in the evil hour when all other possessions became a matter of scramble and pillage. The principle of the guild was a sound principle; and it was the principle and not only the practice that was trampled underfoot . . .

This tragic theme has found memorable expression in such poems as "The Secret People."

> Smile at us, pay us, pass us; but do not quite forget;
> For we are the people of England, that have never spoken yet.

For, equally with Dickens, Mr. Chesterton is the champion of the English poor. In equal degree he is a hater of class and privilege, of cant and bureaucracy. But he is a great demagogue who has been shouted down by Publicity, that "voice loud enough to drown any remarks made by the public." He is the mouthpiece of the poor who cannot hear him. He is their memory and their poet, the cherisher of their traditions stamped out by misery, and the singer of virtues they have almost forgotten. And his sympathies are a proof of his splendid lineage:

> I saw great Cobbett riding,
> The horseman of the shires;
> And his face was red with judgment
> And a light of Luddite fires.

"Cobbett was defeated because the English people was defeated. After the frame-breaking riots, men as men were beaten . . . . . Ireland did not get home rule because England didn't." This instinctive espousal of the cause of the oppressed and of the harassed and pitiable things is nowhere better expressed than in "The Donkey", which needs not quoting. There also will be found that inexpressible and mystic certainty, that the big battalions will one day be confounded by that weak and scattered remnant which has survived a hundred defeats. Yet Mr. Chesterton does not fight with any hope of success, but rather for the continuance of a cause and to witness to a truth:

> In a world of flying loves and fading lusts
> It is something to be sure of a desire.

It is probably his sympathy with the humble yet joyous traditions of England, together with his strong but sensitive feeling for her unrivalled roads and hills and villages, that has contributed to make him subtly and unmistakably English. He is not least English in his deep regard for morals, and a fondness for pertinently pointing morals even about morals: "We have grown to associate morality in a book with a kind of optimism and prettiness; according to us, a moral book is about moral people. But the old idea was almost exactly the opposite; a moral book was about immoral people." We have but to recall Hogarth and Fielding.

But in nothing is the peculiar quality of the autochthonous Englishman seen more clearly than in Mr. Chesterton's patriotism. To people unacquainted with the profound patriotism of Sir Thomas More, Johnson, Cobbett and Dickens, it may be puzzling. For it is anything but an uncritical allegiance to the acts of professional politicians, which Johnson rightly designated as the last refuge of a scoundrel. Nor is it that still more pernicious metaphysical and spiritual perversion that has disfigured Prussia since Frederick.

For he heartily hates what England often seems trying to become, and this produces "a sort of fierce doubt or double-mindedness which cannot exist in vague and homogeneous Englishmen." In his book *The Crimes of England*, he wrote:

> I have passed the great part of my life in criticising and condemning the existing institutions of my country: I think it is infinitely the most patriotic thing a man can do.

The high standard he sets for his own country makes him quick and generous in his recognition of the rights and virtues of others. And the French, American, and Irish peoples have no more discriminating admirer and interpreter than Mr. Chesterton. But like Socrates, he is a gadfly stinging his own countrymen into awareness of the crime of complacency:

> We have made our public schools the strongest walls against a whisper of the honour of England . . . What have we done and where have we wandered, we that have produced sages that could have spoken with Socrates and poets who could walk with Dante, that we should talk as if we had never done anything more intelligent than found colonies and kick niggers?

Mr. Chesterton opposed jingoism at the beginning of the century for the same reason that he opposes pacifism to-day. For both are craven moods that seek the exhilaration or security to be found in mass sentiment and unrealistic unanimity.

He believes in the ordinary man, and in no other sort of man. But unlike another very great journalist, Daniel Defoe, Mr. Chesterton has never failed to pay the ordinary man the compliment of reasoning with him. That is why he is such a poor salesman. For he does not wish to persuade without first convincing. His appeal is always to reason. In fact, that he turns a few cart-wheels out of sheer good spirits by way of enlivening his pages has annoyed a certain type of person, and is sure to puzzle a lazy or fatigued mind. Such, for instance, is his unparalleled power of making verbal coincidences really coincide. But the irreducibly simple language and the appeal to common experience are unmistakably directed to the ordinary person. Mr. T. S. Eliot, writing to the Three Thousand people who comprehend, according to his own computation, the total culture of the West, describes the poet's mind as "being a more finely perfected medium in which special or very varied feelings are at liberty to enter into new combinations." He says no more than Mr. Chesterton before him, who wrote that "nobody believes that an ordinary civilized stockbroker can really produce, out of his own inside, noises which denote all the mysteries of memory and all the agonies of desire." The fact is that Mr. Chesterton has always that additional human energy and intellectual power which constitute humour.

That purely esoteric use of his powers which might have gone to the creation of fine art was made impossible by the appeal of a chaotic and turbid time to his great democratic sympathies. The extraordinary extent of his writing and discussions is proportioned to the desperate need for direction and unity in an age that has "smothered man in men." For external complexity has produced an insane simplification of thought, preying upon personal variety and spontaneous social expression:

We have hands that fashion and heads that know,
But our hearts we lost — how long ago!

What Mr. Chesterton has written of the power of St. Thomas to fix even passing things as they pass, and to scorch details under the magnifying lens of his attention, is strikingly true of himself. His is the power to focus a vast range of material into narrow compass; and his books though very numerous are extremely condensed. They might even be considered as projections of his mastery of epigram and sententious phrase. What had seemed a dull and formless expanse of history is made to shine with contemporary significance, and contemporary details are made to bristle with meaning. It is a great labour of synthesis and reconstruction in which Mr. Chesterton has been engaged. He has fixed his attention on the present and the past, because he is concerned lest our future steps be blindly mistaken. And a strong and growing group of like-minded writers indicates the impression he has made upon his generation. For there are many people who no longer regard Herbert Spencer as a philosopher, or think Mr. Chesterton a medieval buffoon.

Although his thunders of laughter may beguile some readers, there is no more serious master of debate and controversy. When his exuberant fancy may decorate an argument as a gargoyle embellishes a buttress, the buttress is there; and just as the buttress is there, so is the lofty edifice which it supports. There is a perfect continuity between his ideas even when they are most subtle; for he has seen modern problems from the beginning in all their complexity and connexions, in other words, with wisdom. Therefore he has no nostrum and no novelty, no panacea and no private aim; nor is he deceived by his own metaphors. And nothing is more characteristic of him than scrupulous care in the definition of terms.

Mr. Chesterton has commanding vigour of expression, and appreciates the genius of the English language which is full of combative and explosive energy, especially found in short epithets: "A young man grows up in a world that often seems to him to be intolerably old. He grows up among proverbs and precepts that appear to be quite stiff and senseless. He seems to be stuffed with stale things; to be given the stones of death instead of the bread of life; to be fed on the dust of the dead past; to live in a town of tombs." This passage may also be regarded as an instance of what some hold to be Mr. Chesterton's vice of alliteration. But he is doing something quite different from a Swinburne lulling the mind by alliterating woolly, caterpillar words. His energetic hatchet-like phrases hew out sharply defined images that are like a silhouette or a wood-cut. And these are of a piece with the rigorous clarity of his thought.

The artist in Mr. Chesterton has been far from subdued by the philosopher and controversialist. His poetry and his stories are as important as they are popular. It is because they are popular that very little need be said of them just now. But this part of his work is not easily appreciated in isolation from the more abstract portion. For instance, Mr. Chesterton regards the soul of a story as "the ordeal of a free man" . . . . "There is no such thing as a Hegelian story, or a monist story, or a determinist story . . . Every short story does truly begin with the creation and end with the last judgment." The detective story won his praise from the start, because "it is the earliest and only form of popular literature in which is expressed some sense of the poetry of modern life." Such stories are "as rough and refreshing as the ballads of Robin Hood." They are based upon the poetry of fact which Mr. Chesterton has expressed so well. "The romance of the police force is thus the whole romance of man. It is based on the fact that morality is the most dark and daring of conspiracies." That is why the inimitable Father Brown is a psychologist rather than a sleuth; and the culprit he exposes is shown to be a sinner rather than a mere criminal.

The stories of Mr. Chesterton are as colourful melodrama as can be imagined or desired. Like the old melodrama, they display this world as a battlefield and restore the colours to life. They are proof that "the finding and fighting of positive evil is the beginning of all fun and even of all farce." For in *The Napoleon of Notting Hill* and *Manalive* and the others, Mr. Chesterton enters faery lands to show that they are not forlorn. They contain a truly brave new world, rather unlike "the shape of things to come," in which very vivid people are etched upon a background of significantly contrasted colours:

> The broken flowerpot with its red-hot geraniums, the green bulk of Smith and the black bulk of Warner, the blue-spiked railings behind, clutched by the stranger's yellow vulture claws and peered over by his long vulture neck, the silk hat on the gravel and the little cloudlet of smoke floating across the garden as innocently as the puff of a cigarette — all these seemed unnaturally distinct and definite. They existed, like symbols, in an ecstasy of separation.

The most ordinary things become eerily and portentously real. Bodily gestures are stiff with spiritual significance, as in the old pageantry. And the deeps of the subconscious are entered, and monstrous facts from the borderland of the brain impress themselves upon us. As the modern jargon puts it, Mr. Chesterton has achieved an objective correlative for his thought and feeling.

The profound joy in Mr. Chesterton's poems and stories can be properly appreciated only when the suffocating materialism of pre-war days is remembered:

> A cloud was on the mind of men, and wailing went the weather, and
> Life was a fly that faded, and death a drone that stung;
> The world was very old indeed when you and I were young.

But, liberated by faith and joy, Mr. Chesterton represents a very great increase in sensibility over the world that read the *Idylls of the King*. Any valuable extension of awareness is directly determined by the rediscovery of neglected truths, and there is much the same truth behind "The Ballad of the White Horse" and "The Wasteland." Many of Mr. Chesterton's poems have the directness of a shout or a blow, and at times he recaptures the startling simplicity of Chaucer through a combination of sanity and subtlety. Of his inspiriting songs it is unnecessary to speak. They could arouse spirits in a materialist Utopian.

And yet it is no contradiction to say that Mr. Chesterton is primarily an intellectual poet. This is too often overlooked even by those who know that his mind is full of nimble and fiery shapes, and that his wit is "quick, forgetive, apprehensive." He deserves the praise Mr. Eliot affords to Donne for the "quality of transmuting ideas into sensations, of transforming an observation into a state of mind." It is necessary only to refer to the great "Lepanto" or "The Donkey" as perfect achievement of this kind.

Had Mr. Chesterton been merely a quiet intellectual with an ordinary amount of energy, he would certainly have been an artist who was taken seriously by the Three Thousand cultured minds of Europe. The same might be said of Dickens. But in an age of shallow optimism, of crumbling creeds and faltering faith, he has walked securely and wildly, boisterously praising life and heaping benedictions upon decadents. He has become a legend while he yet lives. Nobody could wish him otherwise than as he is.

G. K. Chesterton: A Practical Mystic
Marshall McLuhan - Unbound (11)

ISBN: 1-58423-051-7
Library of Congress Control Number 2005927213

Marshall McLuhan Unbound Project Editors
Eric McLuhan, W. Terrence Gordon

Published in United States in October 2005 by
Gingko Press, Inc.
5768 Paradise Drive, Suite J • Corte Madera, CA 94925
(415) 924-9615 • Fax (415) 924-9608
email: books@gingkopress.com
http://www.gingkopress.com

Design, packaging and production: Die Gestalten Verlag, Berlin
Layout and Typography: onlab, Berlin
Fonts: *Dolly* by Underware, *Bullet* by House Industries
Production: Martin Bretschneider, Vinzenz Geppert
Art direction: Robert Klanten

Made in Germany